W9-BDE-825

A PARRAGON BOOK

Published by Parragon,
13 Whiteladies Road, Clifton,
Bristol BS8 1PB

Produced by The Templar Company plc,
Pippbrook Mill, London Road, Dorking,
Surrey RH4 1JE

Written by Robert Snedden
Consultant: William Crouch
Designed by Mark Summersby

Printed and bound in China

ISBN 0-75252-949-8

FACTFINDERS

HISTORIC
BRITAIN

· PARRAGON ·

CONTENTS

INTRODUCTION

Britain is a country steeped in tradition and history. From stone circles to stately homes, from castles to cathedrals, a wealth of historic sites reflect the rich past of this island nation.

Within the pages of this book are 70 examples of the best that Historic Britain has to offer. There are an enormous variety of sites to choose from in all parts of the country: from Britain's prehistoric past there are ancient stone circles and an Iron Age hillfort; the traces of the once mighty Roman Empire can be found here, as can the ruins of once seemingly impregnable castles and those that still stand firm, evidence of Britain's often troubled past; magnificent abbeys and cathedrals tell of Britain's religious heritage and here, too, are some of the seats of learning and power.

There can be few countries that encompass such a diversity of historical interest within such a small, easily accesible area.

Overleaf is a map showing where the sites detailed within are located. The numbers on the map correspond to page numbers in the book. Why not visit a site near you? There is a lot to discover.

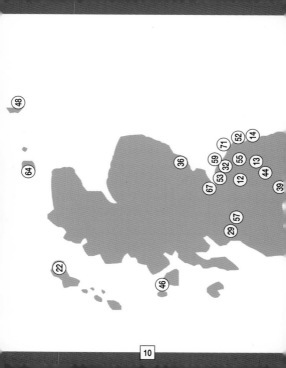

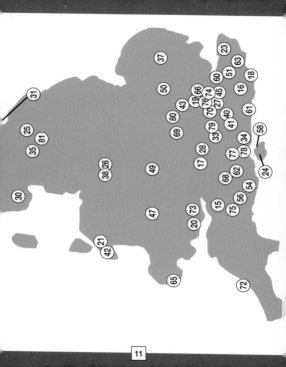

ABBOTSFORD

GALASHIELS, BORDERS

Few houses can express the character of their owner as
well as Abbotsford, home of writer Sir Walter Scott for
the last 20 years of his life. Scott's collection of historic
relics, reflecting his abiding interest in the past, are on
display here, as is his collection of 9000 rare books.
Mementoes of Scottish history such as Rob Roy's
broadsword, a lock of Bonnie Prince Charlie's hair and a
crucifix owned by Mary, Queen of Scots, are all here. The
study where Scott wrote his famous novels can be visited
as can the room where he died.

ALNWICK CASTLE

ALNWICK, NORTHUMBERLAND

The second largest inhabited castle in Britain, after
Windsor Castle, Alnwick Castle dates back to the 12th
century at which time it was a Border stronghold. Stone
soldiers, which can still be seen, were placed along the
ramparts to discourage enemies. The keep and curtain
walls are the oldest sections while the present main building is the result of 18th- and 19th-century reconstruction.
A number of art treasures are housed here, including
works by Canaletto and Titian and a fine collection of
Meissen porcelain.

BAMBURGH CASTLE

BAMBURGH, NORTHUMBERLAND

The mighty stronghold of Bamburgh on a rocky outcrop overlooking the coast is a thrilling sight. The earliest evidence of fortification here dates from the sixth century and the castle keep was built by the Normans. During the Wars of the Roses the castle gained the dubious distinction of being the first to be breached by gunfire. In the 18th century Bamburgh was extensively restored and put to a number of uses including coastguard station, school and hospital. The castle has an impressive collection of 17th-century armour from the Tower of London.

BATH (ROMAN)

BATH, AVON

These baths, constructed around 2000 years ago, are built on the site of the only hot spring in Britain. The spring was a sacred site within the Roman temple of Sulis Minerva. Among the relics on display is a gilded bronze head of the goddess. The spring was used by pilgrims to the temple and by the sick as it was thought to have healing powers. The rectangular swimming bath, fed by water from the spring, is still lined with the original lead. This is the most frequently visited Roman site in Britain. The statues overlooking the bath are Victorian additions.

BATTLE ABBEY

BATTLE, EAST SUSSEX

Battle Abbey was founded by William the Conqueror to give thanks for his victory over Harold Godwinson at Hastings in 1066. The high altar was supposedly erected over the spot where Harold was killed. Little remains of the original church but substantial parts of the 13th-century buildings remain (the abbot's house is now used as a girl's school) and there is a well-preserved 14th-century gatehouse. In the undercroft of the guest house there is a scale model of the Battle of Hastings. It is also possible to walk around the actual battlefield itself.

BLENHEIM PALACE

WOODSTOCK, OXFORDSHIRE

As a reward for his victory over the French at the Battle of Blenheim in 1704, Queen Anne gave the Duke of Marlborough the Royal Manor of Woodstock and money to build a palace. Work was begun on the palace in 1705 by Sir John Vanburgh. Set in a 2100-acre park designed by Capability Brown, the palace features magnificent State Rooms, with fine tapestries and furnishings and, in particular, carvings by Grinling Gibbons. This was the birthplace of Sir Winston Churchill. International Horse Trials are held at the house every September.

BODIAM CASTLE

HASTINGS, KENT

Built between 1385 and 1389, Bodiam Castle is considered by many to be England's finest ruined castle. Massive walls on a rectangular plan, with cylindrical towers at each corner, rectangular towers midway along each of the long walls and gatehouses to the front and rear, make Bodiam a formidable sight. A causeway leads across the moat to a great gatehouse on the castle's north side that still has one of the three original portcullises. The inner court of the castle, the residential area, is in a greater state of ruin than the outer walls and towers.

BUCKINGHAM PALACE

WESTMINSTER, LONDON

The 18th-century Buckingham House was bought by the Crown in 1762 for George III and converted into a palace for George IV by John Nash in 1825. Queen Victoria was the first monarch to make Buckingham Palace her home and in 1847 she added the east front and made some modernisations. Very little alteration has been made to the Palace since that time. Selected rooms in the Palace were first opened to the public in 1993. One of the greatest attractions for the visitor are George IV's State Apartments, built in the 1820s.

CAERLEON

NEWPORT, GWENT

A major Roman legionary garrison was stationed at
Caerleon with thousands of men of the Second Legion
being accommodated on the site. The bath building
uncovered in the 1970s, is the most complete example of
its kind in Britain. The foundations of the barracks and
the remains of the cookhouse have also been found. The
particularly fine amphitheatre nearby was no doubt used
to provide entertainment for the troops. In Caerleon
itself is a museum dedicated to the daily life of the
Roman legionaries.

CAERNARFON CASTLE

CAERNARFON, GWYNEDD

This mighty fortress was begun by Edward I in 1283,
following his defeat of Llywelyn, last of the Welsh
princes, and the work was completed in 1328. The ten-
sided Eagle Tower, with three turrets and a huge eagle
carved on one face, is one of the largest towers built during the medieval period. The infant Edward II, born in
the castle in 1284, was presented to the Welsh people as
the first Prince of Wales. The present Prince of Wales was
invested in a ceremony here in 1969. The Chamberlain
Tower houses the museum of the Royal Welch Fusiliers.

CALLANISH

ISLE OF LEWIS, SCOTLAND

The 4-metre (13-foot) high standing stones of Callanish were erected around 4000 years ago. Thirteen stones stand in a circle, the tallest marking the entrance to a burial cairn within which human bones were found – perhaps the remains of a chieftain. Leading northwards from the inner circle is an avenue of 19 monoliths and further stones lead south, east and west so that the whole site forms a cross. Possibly this was a ceremonial site, or an astronomical observatory or then again, perhaps these were once men, turned to stone by a wrathful sorcerer!

CANTERBURY CATHEDRAL

CANTERBURY, KENT

The Norman Archbishop LeFranc ordered a cathedral to be built here on the ruins of an older Anglo-Saxon building in 1077 to reflect Canterbury's growing importance as a centre of Christianity. Over succeeding centuries the cathedral was added to and rebuilt many times and thus reflects many medieval architectural styles. Canterbury is one of the longest medieval churches in Europe. Perhaps the most important event in its history was the murder of Archbishop Thomas à Becket in the cathedral by Henry II's knights.

CARISBROOKE CASTLE

CARISBROOKE, ISLE OF WIGHT

Carisbrooke Castle is the only medieval castle on the Isle of Wight. Built in the reign of William the Conqueror on the site of a Saxon fort, it is still very well preserved. The 12th-century Norman keep was built on an artificial mound 20 metres (65 feet) high atop a 46-metre (150-foot) hill. The keep also has a 50-metre (160-foot) deep well at the foot of 71 steps. The gatehouse and ramparts are Elizabethan, strengthened in 1588 to meet the threat of the Spanish Armada. Charles I was imprisoned here from 1647-8 before being taken to London for execution.

CASTLE HOWARD

MALTON, NORTH YORKSHIRE

Castle Howard was designed for the 3rd Earl of Carlisle by Sir John Vanburgh at the beginning of the 18th century. A 25-metre (80-foot) dome tops the building's striking facade. Inside is the 59-metre (192-foot) Long Gallery, the Music Room, the Tapestry Room and the Chapel with stained glass windows designed by Edward Burne-Jones in the 19th century. A portrait of Henry VIII by Holbein and works by Gainsborough and Rubens are held here. The family Mausoleum in the grounds was designed by Nicholas Hawksmoor.

CHATSWORTH

CHESTERFIELD, DERBYSHIRE

Work was begun on Chatsworth estate in 1686 on the site of a ruined manor house that had served as a prison for Mary, Queen of Scots. It was designed for the Duke of Devonshire by William Talman, who was also responsible for the baroque interiors. Chatsworth houses an important collection of paintings, furniture and porcelain, including works by Van Dyck and Reynolds. The surrounding parkland, among Britain's finest, was laid out by Capability Brown. The Emperor Fountain in the garden with its 90-metre (290-foot) jet was built for a visit by Czar Nicholas I of Russia that never took place.

CHISWICK HOUSE

CHISWICK, LONDON

The domed mansion of Chiswick House was built between 1725 and 1730 by the 3rd Earl of Burlington. It is considered by many to be one of the finest examples of Palladian architecture in the country. The wonderful interior decoration of the house was designed by William Kent, who also designed the beautiful Italianate gardens that surround the house. Although the gardens have been much reduced in size over the years by encroaching developments many of Kent's classically-influenced statues and his Ionic temple still survive.

CHRIST CHURCH

OXFORD

Originally named Cardinal's College, after its founder, Cardinal Wolsey, who established it in 1525, Christ Church gained its present title in 1546 when the chapel was granted cathedral status. The south, east and west sides of Tom Quad, the great college quadrangle, were started in 1529. A staircase at the southwest corner leads to Wolsey's great hall with its beautiful carved roof. The rebuilt 16th-century gatehouse features a tower designed by Sir Christopher Wren.

Culzean Castle

Ayr, Strathclyde

This grand castle on a clifftop looking out across the Firth of Clyde is the most visited of the National Trust for Scotland's properties. Dating from the 12th century, it was largely rebuilt in 1775 by Robert Adam, who incorporated the old tower into his design. There is much to see, including the massive Oval Staircase under a great glass dome. The castle stands in 560 acres of grounds with terraced gardens. Culzean is pronounced 'Cullane'.

DOVE COTTAGE

GRASMERE, CUMBRIA

The village of Grasmere on the shore of Lake Grasmere in the heart of the Lake District was a favourite place with the Lakeland Poets. Dove Cottage was the home of William Wordsworth (1771-1850) for thirteen years and is now a museum preserving the poet's personal belongings. Wordsworth wrote one of the first guides to the Lake District. He is buried in the village church of St Oswald near the grave of Samuel Taylor Coleridge, another Lakeland Poet. Inside the church there are memorials to Wordsworth and other poets.

DURHAM CATHEDRAL

DURHAM, COUNTY DURHAM

Durham Cathedral dominates the surrounding town from its position above the River Wear. A church was first built here by monks from Lindisfarne, fleeing the Viking raiders, who were in search of a new resting place for St Cuthbert's remains. The Norman bishop William of Calais cleared the site for the building of the present church in 1092. The Norman nave is massive – almost 12 metres (40 feet) wide, 22 metres (72 feet) high and 61 metres (200 feet) long. The Galilee Chapel houses the tomb of the Venerable Bede (died 735), author of the 'Ecclesiastical History of the English People'.

EDINBURGH CASTLE

EDINBURGH, LOTHIAN

Steeped in atmosphere and history, this fortress
dominates the Edinburgh skyline. Castle Rock, the core
of an extinct volcano, rises 133 metres (435 feet) above
sea level and is a formidable natural defence. The oldest
building within the castle grounds is the 12th-century St
Margaret's Chapel on the rock's summit. James IV's
palace in Crown Square houses the Scottish Regalia,
walled up inside the room for over a century after the
Union of Parliaments. The bedroom where James VI of
Scotland and I of England was born can be seen here.

ETON COLLEGE

Henry VI founded Eton College in 1440 to train scholars for King's College, Cambridge, established in the following year. Eton's graduates have included Shelley, Gladstone and the Duke of Wellington. The 15th-century chapel in the Perpendicular style is particularly noteworthy. Within is a superb collection of 15th-century paintings depicting the life of Mary. The red-brick College Hall and the Lower School, built around two quadrangles, also date back to the 15th century with other buildings being later additions.

FISHBOURNE PALACE

FISHBOURNE, WEST SUSSEX

This is the largest Roman residence yet found in Britain.
Why such a magnificently appointed building was
constructed at this location is unknown, though it may
have been built for Cogidubnus, a local king. The palace's
hundred rooms were decorated with mosaic floors and
painted walls and a number of the mosaics
can still be seen in various states of repair. There is a
museum on the site that tells the history of the palace
and the garden has been laid out as it would have been
in the first century AD.

FOUNTAINS ABBEY

RIPON, YORKSHIRE

One of the most spectacular and best preserved abbey
ruins in the whole of Britain, Fountains Abbey was
established by Cistercian monks in 1135 and soon
amassed great wealth. The east end of the church, called
the Chapel of Nine Altars was added in the 13th century
and the graceful tower was added in the early 16th
century just prior to the Dissolution, following which the
abbey was sold by Henry VIII. In 1720 John Aislabie,
Chancellor of the Exchequer, developed the land around
the abbey as the water gardens of Studely Royal.

GLAMIS CASTLE

FORFAR, TAYSIDE

Glamis has been a royal residence since 1372. There was a royal hunting lodge on the site in the 11th century which underwent extensive rebuilding and the present-day castle largely dates from the 15th century. The five-storey L-shaped tower block dates from the 15th century and was redesigned in the 16th century. Many of the castle's rooms are open to the public and an impressive display of furniture, paintings and other objects spanning five centuries can be seen. This was the childhood home of Queen Elizabeth, the Queen Mother.

GRIME'S GRAVE

THETFORD, NORFOLK

This is the largest known flint mine in Britain and it is
formed from a network of hundreds of pits dug between
3000 and 1900BC. The flint mined here would have been
sent in rough, unhewn form to other parts of the country
to be worked into tools such as knives and axeheads.
Vertical shafts lead down to galleries cut through the flint
seams and it is possible for present-day visitors to
descend into the gloom deep beneath the surface to get
some idea of what it must have been like to work the
stone with deer antlers and ox shoulderblades.

HADDON HALL

BAKEWELL, DERBYSHIRE

Haddon Hall, in the midst of the picturesque Peak
District, is possibly the finest example of a medieval
manor house in the country. Work was begun in the 12th
century and the house was expanded in succeeding
centuries. Abandoned in the 18th century, the house was
fully restored in the 1930s. The painted chapel is the oldest part of the house and the Banqueting Hall, with its
minstrels' gallery, the Dining Room and Great Chamber
are also medieval. The 34-metre (110-foot) Long Gallery,
panelled in oak and walnut has a fine decorative ceiling.

HADRIAN'S WALL

NORTHUMBERLAND AND CUMBRIA

Stretching across much of northern England, the wall was
built between AD122 and 128 by the Emperor Hadrian
to mark the frontier between the Roman Empire and the
barbarians of Caledonia to the north. The line of forts
and castles linked by the wall was rebuilt several times in
the next three centuries. One of the main attractions is at
Housesteads, where a Roman infantry cohort was
stationed. Remains of the commandant's house, the
hospital and the four gates can still be seen and there is a
good museum on the site.

HAM HOUSE

RICHMOND, SURREY

Ham House was built around 1610 and redecorated and furnished in the 1670s by the Duke and Duchess of Lauderdale. It is an outstanding example of a house of the Restoration period. Originally designed on an H plan, the house was extended by the Duke and Duchess in 1673 by filling in the uprights of the H on the house's south front. The Lauderdales were great collectors and the house is a treasure trove of Restoration finery, including plasterwork, furniture, wall hangings and works by the artists Kneller and Lely.

HAMPTON COURT PALACE

Hampton Court, begun in 1514 by Cardinal Wolsey, was later acquired by Henry VIII who completed the western portion of the palace, adding the great hall, kitchen and royal tennis courts. The east and south wings were added for William III by Sir Christopher Wren. Attractions include the Tudor kitchens, Henry VIII's State Apartments, woodcarvings by Grinling Gibbons in the Queen's Gallery, paintings by Sir Peter Lely, the maze, laid out during the reign of William III, an Elizabethan knot garden and wrought iron gates by Tijou.

HARLECH CASTLE

HARLECH, GWYNEDD

One of Edward I's castles, Harlech was built between 1283 and 1290. Skilled workmen were brought at great expense from all parts of England to ensure the speedy completion of the work. A sheer drop to the sea once protected the castle but today the coast has advanced and the castle stands above the dunes. In 1404 Owain Glyndwr starved the castle's defenders into submission and adopted it as his headquarters for the next five years. Fifty soldiers, the famous 'Men of Harlech', held the castle during a lengthy siege in the Wars of the Roses.

HATFIELD HOUSE

HATFIELD, HERTFORDSHIRE

Hatfield is a particularly fine example of a Jacobean house. It was built by Robert Cecil between 1607 and 1611, during the reign of James I. The inside of the house is impressive and contains a number of fine paintings, including a famous portrait of Elizabeth I by Nicholas Hilliard. Many other relics associated with Elizabeth are held here and in the grounds of the house stand the remains of Hatfield Palace where she spent much of her childhood. Most of the palace was torn down by Cecil to provide materials for his new house.

HAWORTH

WEST YORKSHIRE

The Brontë Parsonage Museum at Haworth was the
home of the famous Brontë family from 1820 to 1861.
The house was built in 1778-79 and the decoration is just
as it was in the 1850s. Manuscripts and books of the
novelist sisters. Charlotte, Emily and Anne are on display
here, as are their furniture, personal mementoes and let-
ters to friends. The bleak Yorkshire moors, which
inspired much of their writing, including *Jane Eyre* and
Wuthering Heights, are close to the house and it is
possible to retrace some of the sisters' favourite walks.

HOUSES OF PARLIAMENT

WESTMINSTER, LONDON

Work on rebuilding the Palace of Westminster, as it is also known, was begun in 1840 after the original building was destroyed by fire in 1834. The Victorian Gothic style was chosen to blend with nearby Westminster Abbey. Augustus Pugin was responsible for most of the decorative detail. This is where the legislative chambers of the Parliament meet – the House of Commons and the House of Lords. Visitors can watch debates from the Strangers' Gallery – apply first to your MP or embassy. The clock tower houses Big Ben, a 13.5 ton bell.

IONA ABBEY

IONA, STRATHCLYDE

This peaceful island off the coast of Mull was where St
Columba built his monastery when he arrived from
Ireland in AD563 to convert the heathen Picts to his
Celtic brand of Christianity. The cathedral, much restored
and renovated, dates from around 1500. Three ancient
Celtic crosses stand outside the cathedral. Many of the
ancient kings of Scotland are reputed to have been
buried here, including Macbeth and Duncan. On a low
hill overlooking the cathedral are the remains of a small
drystone cell, perhaps Columba's sleeping place.

IRONBRIDGE GORGE

TELFORD, SHROPSHIRE

Ironbridge Gorge was one of the most important centres of activity in the Industrial Revolution. There are many attractions here, bringing to life a fascinating period in history, including the Museum of Iron, the Coalport China Museum and the open-air Blists Hill Museum, which recreates a 19th-century community, complete with church, baker, pharmacy, pub and a working foundry producing wrought iron. The bridge itself was the first iron bridge in the world, built by Abraham Darby III in 1779.

JARLSHOF

SUMBURGH, SHETLAND

There were settlements on this site almost continuously from the late Stone Age around 2000BC to the late-16th-century Earls of Orkney. The Bronze Age dwellings were built in the style of Minoan Crete. The remains of the various settlements are spread over the promontory. Displays will help you to interpret the site. The Bronze Age village includes a metal workshop and there are two Iron Age earth houses and a broch (a round stone tower). A number of longhouses remain from the time of the Viking occupation. A museum exhibits some of the artefacts that have been uncovered from the site.

KENILWORTH CASTLE

KENILWORTH, WARWICKSHIRE

The grandeur of its ruins has made Kenilworth one of the most visited of Britain's historic sites. The massive rectangular keep, with walls nearly 6 metres (20 feet) thick in places, was probably built in the 12th century and various additions were made over the succeeding 400 years or so. John of Gaunt built the great hall and the Strong Tower in the 14th century. In 1575, Robert Dudley, Earl of Leicester, laid on an extravagant entertainment for Elizabeth I that lasted 19 days and became legendary for its prodigal waste.

KING'S COLLEGE

CAMBRIDGE

King's College was founded in 1441 by Henry VI for the further education of the students of Eton College, founded by the king in the previous year. King's College Chapel, on the north side of the great court, was started by Henry VI and completed by Henry VIII. It is reckoned by many to be the finest example of Perpendicular architecture in Britain. The outside of the building features elegant stone buttress pinnacles, while inside there are splendid stained glass windows and high fan-vaulted ceilings. The altarpiece is by Rubens.

LEEDS CASTLE

MAIDSTONE, KENT

Described as 'the loveliest castle in the world', Leeds
Castle is built on two islands in the middle of a lake and
stands amidst 500 acres of parkland featuring extensive
greenhouses, aviaries, woodland gardens and a vineyard.
The gardens were designed by Capability Brown. Within
the castle, among other, more usual, treasures, can be
found a museum of medieval dog collars! The site of a
Saxon manor in the ninth century, the castle was built in
1120 and converted into a palace by Henry VIII and
became the home of his first wife, Catherine of Aragon.

LINDISFARNE PRIORY

HOLY ISLAND, NORTHUMBERLAND

The monastery of Lindisfarne was founded in the seventh century by St Aidan and monks from Iona. From here, Christianity spread to northern England and the monastery became a centre of learning. The wonderful Lindisfarne Gospels (now in the British Museum) were produced here. The monastery was abandoned in the ninth century following Viking raids. The priory ruins that stand on the site today date from the 11th century, with the most substantial remains being those of the 12th-century west front and tower.

LINLITHGOW PALACE

LINLITHGOW, LOTHIAN

Picturesquely situated on the edge of Linlithgow Loch,
the ruined royal palace of Linlithgow is one of Scotland's
most visited sites. Most of the remaining building was
commissioned by James IV in 1425 although work carried
out on behalf of James I and James III can also be seen.
The palace was gutted by fire in 1746 and only a shell
remains. This was the birthplace of Mary, Queen of Scots,
in 1542. The restored fountain in the courtyard was a
wedding present from her father, James V, to his wife,
Mary of Guise, in 1538.

MAIDEN CASTLE

DORCHESTER, DORSET

This Iron Age hill fort is one of Europe's finest.
Extensive earthwork fortifications cover 47 acres and the
outer perimeter stretches for 3km (2 miles). Grain
storage pits have been found on the site and it is likely
that it was constructed to defend supplies from raiders.
Evidence of occupation has been found dating back to
around 2000BC with work on the fort being carried out
between 700 and 100BC. The burial ground of the
defenders who fell when the castle was captured by the
Romans in AD43 was discovered in the 1930s.

MELROSE ABBEY

MELROSE, BORDERS

The beautiful ruins of Melrose Abbey give some idea of what a magnificent place it must have been when it was complete. It was founded by David I in 1136 and suffered great damage at the hands of Edward II in 1322 and Richard II in 1385. It was finally destroyed by the Duke of Somerset in 1547. Most of the present remains can be dated to a 15th-century reconstruction. The heart of Robert the Bruce is reputed to be buried somewhere here, perhaps under the floor of the chapter house.

MONTACUTE HOUSE

YEOVIL, SOMERSET

An Elizabethan house built of honey-brown Ham Hill stone in the 1590s by Sir Edward Phelips, who became Speaker of the House of Commons in 1604. The windows and rounded gables in the Flemish style date from this time, but the fluted columns and heraldic beasts are 18th-century additions. Within, the house features decorated ceilings, ornate fireplaces and a wonderful collection of heraldic stained glass and 16th-century wood panelling. In the Long Gallery there is a display of Tudor and Jacobean portraits from the National Portrait Gallery.

NEW LANARK

The village of New Lanark on the banks of the River
Clyde was founded in 1785 by industrialist David Dale to
provide homes for the workers in its textile mills. The
social reformer Robert Owen became a partner in New
Lanark in 1800 and with Dale he set up many welfare
schemes for the workers, including a reduction in the
working day to 10.5 hours and the introduction of some
of Britain's first infant schools. The village is now
preserved as a museum and offers a fascinating insight
into 19th-century working life.

OSBORNE HOUSE

ISLE OF WIGHT

Osborne House was built by Queen Victoria in 1845 as a seaside residence. Albert, the Prince Consort, was in large part responsible for the design of the house, working in conjunction with the builder Thomas Cubitt. Victoria spent most of her time at Osborne and died here in 1901. The Queen's apartments have been preserved more or less as she left them and are filled with furniture and everyday objects that are typical of the period that bears her name. The gardens feature a miniature fort and a Swiss cottage, built by Albert for the royal children.

PALACE OF HOLYROODHOUSE

EDINBURGH, LOTHIAN

James IV, who instigated much of the building of
Edinburgh Castle, enlarged the guesthouse of the Abbey
of Holyrood as his Edinburgh residence around 1500.
The picture gallery displays portraits of Scottish
monarchs, many of which are entirely imaginary. Next to
the palace are the ruins of Holyrood Abbey, founded in
1128 by David I. A fragment of the True Cross (the Holy
Rood) was supposedly brought here in the 11th century
by Queen Margaret. The palace is closed to visitors when
members of the Royal Family are in residence.

ROCHESTER CASTLE

ROCHESTER, KENT

Work on the castle began in 1087, soon after the Norman Conquest, to guard a crossing over the River Medway and it became an important royal stronghold for several centuries. The massive four-storeyed square keep was built between 1127 and 1135 and is over 30 metres (100 feet) high with 4-metre (13-foot) thick walls. Fine views over the surrounding town and countryside can be had from the top. The south-east corner was rebuilt after it had been mined by King John in 1216 to end a seven-week siege during his war against rebel barons.

ROYAL PAVILION

BRIGHTON, SUSSEX

The former seaside residence of George IV has been described as the most extraordinary palace in Europe. The original house by Henry Holland was rebuilt in an Indian-influenced style by John Nash between 1815 and 1820 as a summer palace for the then Prince Regent. The spires were intended to represent Crusader tents. The onion domes are a later addition. The music room and banqueting room, also designed by Nash, mix Chinese and Gothic styles. Fine Regency furniture is displayed throughout the richly decorated state rooms. The gardens have recently been restored to the original Regency plan.

SALISBURY CATHEDRAL

SALISBURY, WILTSHIRE

The interior of Salisbury Cathedral is unique in that it is the only cathedral in Britain to be designed in the same style, having been built in just 38 years between 1220 and 1258. The cathedral is light and airy inside, with numerous windows. The chapter house has an impressive collection of books and manuscripts, including a copy of the Magna Carta. Also within the cathedral is a clock dating from 1386, the oldest working example in Britain. The cathedral spire, at 123 metres (404 feet) high is the tallest in Britain.

SISSINGHURST

SISSINGHURST, KENT

The writer Vita Sackville-West and her husband, Sir
Harold Nicholson, bought the neglected Tudor mansion
of Sissinghurst Castle in 1930 and set about restoring it.
The gardens are now among the most famous in the
country and are a popular attraction. Sackville-West
divided the garden into different areas with hedgerows.
Each area has a theme so that, for example, there is a
Summer Garden, a White Garden and Cottage Garden.
The rose garden has many examples of old-fashioned
varieties and there is a well-stocked herb garden.

SKARA BRAE

STROMNESS, ORKNEY

A late Neolithic village that remained buried from sight for around 4000 years until a storm uncovered it, Skara Brae provides a unique insight into Stone Age life. The village was constructed on two levels with part of the settlement on higher ground for summer occupation and another, deeper and more sheltered level for use when the weather was harsh. Excavation has brought to light several of the one-roomed houses that made up the village. Most things were of stone, including stone beds, tables and cupboards and stone boxes for keeping fish.

ST DAVID'S CATHEDRAL

ST DAVID'S, DYFED

St David's is Britain's smallest city. A community was
founded here by St David, patron saint of Wales, around
550. The present cathedral was built in the 12th century
in a hollow below the town and is the largest in Wales.
Inside the cathedral is a shrine to the saint dating from
1275, the original having been stolen in 1089, a wonderful
14th-century rood screen separating the nave and the
choir and the tomb of a knight, thought to be a 12th-
century Welsh prince. Nearby are the ruins of the 13th-
century Bishop's Palace.

St Paul's Cathedral

City of London

St Paul's Cathedral is perhaps Sir Christopher Wren's greatest achievement. It was built to replace the original cathedral, destroyed by the Great Fire of London in 1666. Completed in 1710, the new St Paul's is magnificent. At 111 metres (360 feet) the dome is one of the highest in the world – the acoustics of the Whispering Gallery are remarkable. The choir stalls were carved by Grinling Gibbons and the ironwork, particularly the great wrought iron gates, is the work of Jean Tijou. The west front of the cathedral is strongly Classical in style.

STIRLING CASTLE

STIRLING, CENTRAL

Perched on a 77-metre (250-foot) basalt rock outcrop, Stirling Castle's strategic position at the highest navigable point on the River Forth and on the road to the Highlands has made it the scene of many important events in Scottish history. Seven battlefields can be seen from the castle. The present building dates from the 15th and 16th centuries and its features include 17th-century frescoes in the Chapel Royal and the Stirling Heads, a collection of 38 roundels in the Palace, thought to depict members of the royal court.

STONEHENGE

WILTSHIRE

The great stone circle of Stonehenge is perhaps the greatest monument to Bronze Age ingenuity in Europe. Work on the site began some 5000 years ago, the earliest parts being the encircling ditch and embankment. Some 700 years later 80 two-ton blue stones were brought here from south Wales. Then the even more massive 50-ton Sarsen stones were moved from the Marlborough Downs and the site took on the form we recognize today. Clearly this must have been a site of great significance to the people who undertook such a massive task.

STOWE GARDENS

STOWE, BUCKINGHAMSHIRE

The 18th-century landscaped gardens of Stowe have been described as Britain's largest work of art. They feature the largest number of garden buildings in England, by Vanburgh, Gibbs and Kent, who designed the Elysian Fields, the Grecian Fields and other prospects in a natural style, flying in the face of convention, which, at the time, was for a more formal layout. Capability Brown and Robert Adam made some later modifications. Stowe House, formerly the home of the Duke of Buckingham, which stands within the grounds, is now a public school.

SYON HOUSE

ISLEWORTH, LONDON

In 1750, Robert Adam was commissioned by the 1st
Duke of Northumberland to renovate the mansion of
Syon House. The result is a breathtaking example of
Adam at his finest. The Red Drawing Room, the Long
Gallery and the Great Hall were all furnished and
sumptuously decorated by Adam. The garden was land-
scaped by Capability Brown, but only the elongated lake
survives from his original conception. In Syon Park is the
huge metal and glass Great Conservatory, designed by
Fowler in 1829, the first construction of its kind.

TANTALLON CASTLE

NORTH BERWICK, LOTHIAN

Tantallon, facing out across the rocky shore of the Firth
of Forth, was the stronghold in the 14th century of the
Douglasses, who frequently rebelled against the Scottish
king. Twice the Scots besieged the castle, in 1491 and
1528, but without success. The castle finally succumbed to
General Monk's forces in 1651 after a 12-day bombard-
ment. In 1699 the Douglasses sold the castle and the
building fell into ruin. The main castle defences faced in
towards the headland, the cliffs presenting an
impregnable defence on the seaward side.

TINTAGEL CASTLE

TINTAGEL, CORNWALL

That this atmospheric and dramatic site was the legendary birthplace of King Arthur was first recorded in Geoffrey of Monmouth's entirely fictitious *History of the Kings of Britain* in 1136. The castle was built for the Earl of Cornwall in 1145, who may have been inspired by the Arthurian legend. It fell into disuse some 300 years later and was in ruins by Tudor times. The castle is said to be on the site of a Celtic monastery founded around AD500 and evidence has also been found of a fifth- to eighth-century stronghold here.

TINTERN ABBEY

CHEPSTOW, GWENT

Magnificent soaring arches and fine stonework make Tintern one of the most beautiful of Britain's ruined abbeys. It is one of the best known, and most frequently visited of such sites. It was founded as a Cistercian monastery in 1131 but the present day ruins date almost entirely from rebuilding carried out at the end of the 13th century. Most of the buildings, with the exception of the monastery church, were destroyed during the Dissolution.

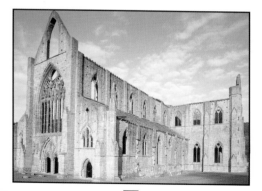

TOWER OF LONDON

CITY OF LONDON

The White Tower at the centre of this famous castle was
built by William the Conqueror around 1078 as a fortress
from which he could exert his control over London. In
the course of its history the Tower has been fortress,
palace and prison. Sir Walter Ralegh was imprisoned in
the Tower for 13 years and two of Henry VIII's wives
were executed here. From the reign of Charles II until
1812 this was the headquarters of the Royal Mint. Today
it is the home of the Crown Jewels and Regalia, and the
famous Yeoman Warders, or Beefeaters.

WELLS CATHEDRAL

WELLS, SOMERSET

Wells is one of the most beautiful of England's cathedrals. Work on the present church was started around 1175. Among the many fine features are the octagonal Chapter House, reached by a well-worn, although still impressive staircase; the central tower in the Decorated style, supported by a unique pair of double arches; the cathedral library; and a 14th-century clock. On the outside of the church, the west front has 300 niches each containing a life-size statue sculpted in the 13th century.

WESTMINSTER ABBEY

WESTMINSTER, LONDON

Edward the Confessor founded a church here in 1065 to provide a place for his burial. Henry III began to rebuild the church in the 13th century and much additional work was carried out in succeeding centuries, including the 68-metre (223-feet) high towers of the west facade built by Nicholas Hawksmoor in 1740. Almost all of England's rulers from Henry III to George II are buried in the abbey and coronations and important royal weddings are held here. Celebrated Britons, including Henry Purcell, Charles Darwin and Isaac Newton, are commemorated.

WINCHESTER CATHEDRAL

WINCHESTER, HAMPSHIRE

Work was begun on the cathedral in 1079 but of that original building only the crypt and the massive transepts remain. Other parts of the church are in a variety of styles, including the Decorated choir, which features the oldest carved wooden stalls in England, dating from the 14th century. The massive nave, built by William of Wykeham, also dates from this period. The cathedral library holds an important collection of over 4000 books, including the exquisitely illuminated 12th-century Winchester Bible.

WINCHESTER COLLEGE

WINCHESTER, HAMPSHIRE

Winchester College was founded by William of
Wykeham, Bishop of Winchester, in 1382 and is the
oldest public school in England. Two of the original
houses, Flint Court and Chamber Court, built between
1387 and 1394, still stand – Seventh Chamber, is the oldest schoolroom in the country. The college chapel has
windows in the Perpendicular style, with much of the
original medieval stained glass preserved, and a fan-
vaulted timber roof used by Henry VI as a model for
Eton College's chapel. The great tower dates from 1481.

WINDSOR CASTLE

WINDSOR, BERKSHIRE

Windsor is the largest inhabited castle in the world.
William the Conqueror built a wooden fort on the site
and over the centuries almost every other monarch has
made some addition to the structure. Extensive
alterations were made during the reigns of Charles II and
George IV. St George's Chapel, begun by Edward IV and
completed by Henry VIII is a magnificent building with
intricate carvings and wonderful fan vaulting. The State
Rooms contain many fine examples of furnishings and
paintings, including works by Van Dyck and Rembrandt.

WOBURN ABBEY

LEIGHTON BUZZARD, BEDFORDSHIRE

This site has been the home of the Dukes of Bedford
since 1547. The original Woburn Abbey was a Cistercian
monastery built on the site in 1145 but closed by Henry
VIII during the Dissolution. The present house, one of
the great stately homes of England, was built in 1744 and
remodelled in 1802. Woburn has a notable collection of
the works of Sir Joshua Reynolds, works by Canaletto,
Van Dyck and Rembrandt, and an extensive display of
French and English 18th-century furniture. Nine species
of deer roam freely in the Deer Park.

YORK MINSTER

YORK, YORKSHIRE

Work on this, the largest Gothic church in England, began in 1220 and was not completed for another 250 years. For this reason York Minster reflects a variety of architectural styles, from the Norman crypt at the east end to the early 15th-century central tower. Standing beneath the tower it is possible to see three great periods of Gothic architecture. The Minster houses the largest collection of medieval stained glass in Britain, including the largest single sheet and a panel that is perhaps the oldest in the country (c.1150).

TIMELINE OF HISTORY

c.6000BC At the end of the last ice age, the English Channel forms, separating Britain from continental Europe

3500BC Stone circles are erected around Britain

3000BC Work begins on Stonehenge

2100BC Bronze Age culture reaches Britain

1000BC Settled agricultural communities appear

550BC The Celts reach Britain from southern Europe

500BC The Iron Age begins

150BC Peoples from Gaul migrate to Britain

55BC Julius Caesar lands in Britain

AD43 Claudius invades; Britain becomes part of the Roman Empire

c.AD50 The foundation of London

61 Boudicca leads rebellion against the Romans

122 Hadrian's Wall is begun on border with Scotland

143 Romans occupy southern Scotland and begin Antonine Wall

206 Tribes from Scotland attack Hadrian's Wall

254 St Alban becomes Britain's first Christian martyr

367 The Picts overrun Hadrian's Wall

410 End of Roman rule in Britain

440-450 Invasions by Angles, Saxons and Jutes

c.450 Saxons first settle in Kent

c.527 The Saxon kingdoms of Essex and Middlesex are established

c.556 Saxons set up seven kingdoms across Britain

563 St Columba lands on Iona
c.607 The first St Paul's Church is built in London
635 St Aidan founds Lindisfarne monastery
c.783 Offa of Mercia completes his dyke separating England and Wales
787 The first Viking raids on Britain
793 The first Viking raids on Lindisfarne and Jarrow
795 The Danes attack Iona
c.850 Kenneth Macalpine becomes king of all Scotland
865 The Danish Great Army lands
867 Northumbria falls to the Danes
870 East Anglia falls to the Danes
874 Mercia falls to the Danes
876 The Danish kingdom of York is established
893 Alfred the Great inaugurates the Royal Navy
910-920 Edward the Elder recaptures most of the Danelaw
937 Athelstan defeats Norse, Scots and Strathclyde Welsh at Brunanburh to become king of all England
1002 Ethelred orders the massacre of all Danes in England
1003 King Swein of Denmark invades
1013 Swein returns; the Danelaw accepts him as king
1014 Death of Swein; the Danish army elect Cnut as king
1016 Cnut defeats Edmund Ironside to become king of all England
1065 Westminster Abbey is consecrated
1066 (September) King Harold defeats and kills Harold of Norway at Stamford Bridge

1066 (October) The Norman Conquest: Duke William of Normandy defeats and kills King Harold of England at the Battle of Hastings

1066 (December) William is crowned king

1071 Hereward the Wake is defeated at Ely bringing to an end the resistance to the Normans

1078 William begins the Tower of London

1086 The Domesday survey is carried out

1106 Henry I conquers Normandy

1139-53 Civil war in England

1141-45 Geoffrey of Anjou conquers Normandy

1153 Henry of Anjou (later Henry II) invades England

1162 Thomas à Becket becomes archbishop of Canterbury

1169-72 English conquest of Ireland begins

1170 Murder of Archbishop Becket by Henry II's knights

1215 Magna Carta signed by King John

1282-83 Edward I conquers Wales

1295 Alliance between France and Scotland

1296 Edward I invades Scotland but meets stiff resistance

1297 William Wallace defeats the English at Stirling

1298 Edward I defeats Wallace at Falkirk

1306 Rebellion of Robert the Bruce

1314 Robert the Bruce defeats Edward II at Bannockburn

1337 The Hundred Years War with France begins

1347 The English capture Calais

1348 Plague first reaches England

1381 The Peasants' Revolt

1415 The English win the Battle of Agincourt

1419-20 England conquers Normandy

1449-50 France recaptures Normandy

1453 The Hundred Years War with France comes to an end

1455 The Wars of the Roses begin

1485 The War of the Roses ends with the Battle of Bosworth

1512 England at war with France and Scotland

1513 Defeat of Scots at Battle of Flodden

1535 Act of Union joins England and Wales

1536 The Dissolution of the Monasteries

1542 Engish defeat invading Scottish army at Solway Moss

1585 England at war with Spain

1587 Mary, Queen of Scots, is executed

1588 Defeat of the Spanish Armada

1603 The Union of Crowns; James VI of Scotland becomes James I of England

1605 The Gunpowder Plot

1607 The settlement of Virginia

1620 The Pilgrim Fathers sail to New England

1629 Charles I dissolves Parliament

1642 Civil War

1644 Parliamentary armies win decisive Battle of Marston Moor

1648 Second Civil War

1649 Charles I executed – England becomes a republic

1649-53 England governed by the Rump Parliament

1649-50 Oliver Cromwell conquers Ireland

1650-52 Oliver Cromwell conquers Scotland
1653 Cromwell dissolves the Rump Parliament and becomes Lord Protector
1655-60 War with Spain
1657 Cromwell rejects kingship
1659 Cromwell's son overthrown by the army
1660 Charles II restored
1665 The Great Plague
1666 The Great Fire of London
1688 William of Orange invades – James II flees
1690 William III defeats Irish and French army at the Battle of the Boyne
1694 Bank of England founded
1704 Britain captures Gibraltar from Spain
1707 The Union of England and Scotland
1715 First Jacobite rebellion fails
1745 Second Jacobite rebellion fails
1746 Battle of Culloden
1776 American Declaration of Independence
1781 American troops defeat the British at Yorktown
1788 The first convict ships sail to Australia
1801 Union with Ireland
1803 The Napoleonic Wars begin
1805 Nelson defeats French and Spanish fleets at Trafalgar
1815 Napoleon is defeated at the Battle of Waterloo
1834 Slavery abolished in the British Empire
1854-6 The Crimean War
1876 Victoria is proclaimed Empress of India

1880-81 First Boer War
1882 Britain occupies Egypt
1899-1902 Second Boer War
1903 The Suffragette Movement is founded
1908 Old Age Pensions are introduced
1914 First World War begins
1916 Battle of the Somme
1917 Battle of Passchendaele
1918 End of First World War
1919 Women over 30 get the vote for the first time
1926 The General Strike
1928 Vote given to everyone over 21
1936 First television transmissions
1939 Second World war begins
1940 The Battle of Britain
1942 Montgomery's army defeats the Germans at El Alamein
1943 Allies invade Italy
1944 D-Day landings at Normandy
1945 Second World War ends. Massive Labour General Election victory
1946 The National Health Service is set up
1956 Anglo-French troops invade Suez
1959 Oil is discovered in the North sea
1973 Britain enters the Common Market
1979 Margaret Thatcher becomes first woman Prime Minister of Britain
1982 War with Argentina over the Falkland Islands
1994 Channel Tunnel links Britain to continental Europe.

ROYAL BRITAIN

Monarchs of Scotland

Kenneth Macalpine	(843–858)
Donald	(858–862)
Constantine	(862–877)
Aed	(877–878)
Eochaid and Giric	(878–889)
Donald II	(889–900)
Constantine II	(900–943)
Malcolm I	(943–954)
Indulf	(954–962)
Dubh	(62–966)
Culen	(966–971)
Kenneth II	(971–995)
Constantine III	(995–997)
Kenneth III	(997–1005)
Malcolm II	(1005–1034)
Duncan I	(1034–1040)
Macbeth	(1040–1057)
Lulach	(1058)

James V . . . . (1513–1542)
Mary . . . . (1542–1567)
James VI (James I of England). (1567– 1625)

Monarchs of England and Britain

Athelstan (first king of all England) (924–939)
Edmund I . . . . (939–946)
Eadred. . . . . (946–955)
Eadwig. . . . . (955–959)
Edgar. . . . . (959–975)
Edward the Martyr. . . . . (975–979)
Ethelred the Unready. . . . . . (979–1016)
Edmund II . . . . (1016)
Cnut I. . . . . (1016–1035)
Harold I . . . . (1037–1040)
Harthacnut . . . . (1040–1042)
Edward the Confessor . . . . (1042–1066)
Harold II. . . . . (1066)
William I (the Conqueror) . (1066–1087)
William II . . . . (1087–1100)
Henry I . . . . (1100–1135)

```
Stephen . . . . . . . . . . . . . . . . (1135–1154)
Henry II. . . . . . . . . . . . . . . (1154–1189)
Richard I (the Lionheart). . (1189–1199)
John . . . . . . . . . . . . . . . . . . (1199–1216)
Henry III . . . . . . . . . . . . . . (1216–1272)
Edward I . . . . . . . . . . . . . . . (1272–1307)
Edward II . . . . . . . . . . . . . . (1307–1327)
Edward III. . . . . . . . . . . . . . (1327–1377)
Richard II . . . . . . . . . . . . . . (1377–1399)
Henry IV . . . . . . . . . . . . . . . (1399–1413)
Henry V. . . . . . . . . . . . . . . . (1413–1422)
Henry VI . . (1422–1461 and 1470–1471)
Edward IV . . . . . . . . . . . . . . (1461–1483)
Edward V (never crowned) . . . . . (1483)
Richard III. . . . . . . . . . . . . . (1483–1485)
Henry VII . . . . . . . . . . . . . . (1485–1509)
Henry VIII . . . . . . . . . . . . . (1509–1547)
Edward VI. . . . . . . . . . . . . . (1547–1553)
Mary I . . . . . . . . . . . . . . . . (1553–1558)
Elizabeth I. . . . . . . . . . . . . . (1558–1603)
James I (James VI of Scotland) . . (1603–1625)
```

```
Charles I . . . . . . . . . . . . . . (1625–1649)
The Interregnum –
Oliver Cromwell  . . . . . . . . (1649– 1658)
Charles II. . . . . . . . . . . . . . (1660–1685)
James II . . . . . . . . . . . . . . . (1685–1688)
William III . . . . . . . . . . (1689–1702) and
Mary II  . . . . . . . . . . . . . . (1689–1694)
Anne  . . . . . . . . . . . . . . . . . (1702–1714)
George I  . . . . . . . . . . . . . . (1714–1727)
George II. . . . . . . . . . . . . . (1727–1760)
George III . . . . . . . . . . . . . (1760–1820)
George IV  . . . . . . . (Regent: 1811–1820,
                        Monarch 1820–1830)
William IV. . . . . . . . . . . . . (1830–1837)
Victoria  . . . . . . . . . . . . . . . (1837–1901)
Edward VII . . . . . . . . . . . . (1901–1910)
George V. . . . . . . . . . . . . . . (1910–1936)
Edward VIII . . . . . . . (1936 – abdicated)
George VI . . . . . . . . . . . . . (1936–1952)
Elizabeth II  . . . . . . . . . . . . . . . (1952– )
```

Photographic Acknowledgements

Bruce Coleman Limited

pp.14, 18 Eric Crichton, p.19 Peter Terry, p.21 Geoff Doré, p.22 Chris James, p.24 Eric Crichton, p.26 Chris James, p.27 Eric Crichton, p.30 Andy Price, p.31 Eric Crichton, p.32 Bruce Coleman Ltd, p.35 Eric Crichton, p.37 Geoff Doré, p.39 Wild-Type Productions, pp.40, 41 Eric Crichton, pp.46, 48 Allan G. Potts, p.51 Rod Williams, p.56 Eric Crichton, p.60 Peter Terry, pp.61,62 Eric Crichton, p.63 Jennifer Fry, p.64 Chris James, p.68 Geoff Doré, p.71 Allan G. Potts, p.72 Nigel Blake, p.73 Eric Crichton, p.75 John Worrall, p.78 Eric Crichton.

Robert Harding Picture Library

p.12 Michael Jenner, p.13 Roy Rainford, p.15 Robert Harding, p.16 Adam Woolfitt, p17 Robert Harding, p.20 Michael Jenner, p.23 John Miller, p.25 Rolf Richardson, p.28 Philip Craven, p.29 Michael Jenner, p.33 N. Boyd, p.34 Robert Harding, p.36 Adam Woolfitt, p.38 Robert Harding, p.42 Nigel Francis, p.43 Robert Harding, p.44 Gascoigne, p.45 Robert Harding, p.47 Peter Scholey, p.49 Martin F. Chillmaid, p.50 Nigel Francis, p.52 Robert Harding, p.53 Philip Craven, p.54 Roy Rainford, p.55 Robert Harding, p.57 Michael Jenner, p.58 Robert Harding, pp.59, 65 Philip Craven, p.66 Walter Rawlings, p.67 Michael Jenner, p.69 L. Proud, p.70 A.R. Lampshire, p.74 Roy Rainford, p.76 Robert Harding, p.78 David Lomax, p.79 Philip Craven, p.80 Robert Harding, p.81 Adam Woolfitt.

TITLES IN THIS SERIES INCLUDE:

ASTRONOMY

CARD GAMES

CLANS & TARTANS

FASTEST CARS

FLAGS OF THE WORLD

HANDGUNS & SMALL ARMS

HISTORIC BRITAIN

HUMAN BODY

INVENTIONS

NATURAL DISASTERS